SAY IT, BELIEVE IT, BE IT

REFLECTIVE AFFIRMATIONS JOURNAL

For Soul Healing, Relationships, Personal Transformation, and Success

Shaunté L. Chandler

Copyright © 2022 by Shaunté L. Chandler

Published by Shaunté L. Chandler in Partnership with
Bold Publishing

(https://denisenicholson.com/bold-publishing)

Book Cover by: Bold Publishing
Book Layout by: Opeyemi Ikuborije

Publisher's Note:

Without limiting the rights under copyright reserved above, no part of this publication may be reproduced, stored in or introduced into a retrieval system, or transmitted, in any form, or by any means (electronic, mechanical, photocopying, recording, or otherwise), without the prior written permission of both the copyright owner and the publisher of the book.

Manufactured in the United States of America

ISBN: 978-1-7363853-8-8

Library of Congress Control Number: 2022905779

website: www.essenceoflifehwc.com

CONTENTS

Acknowledgment . . . . *iv*

Introduction . . . . *v*

Inner Reflections Affirmations Journey Section One: 1

    Affirmations for Soul Healing *1*

Inner Reflections Affirmations Journey Section Two: 51

    Affirmations for Relationships *51*

Inner Reflections Affirmations Journey Section Three: 101

    Affirmations for Transformation *101*

Inner Reflections Affirmations Journey Section Four: 151

    Affirmations for Success *151*

Acknowledgment

A heartfelt thank you to all my spiritual, business, and personal development coaches and mentors who believed in me and my vision.

Introduction

The words you say and think shape your reality. Affirmations are positive phrases; seeds for the subconscious mind. By reprogramming the subconscious mind, you shift your life's paradigms and begin transforming your reality. However, affirmations alone do not cause drastic life changes. You must internalize the affirmations, you must believe and feel what you are saying. In addition, you can internalize affirmations by reflecting on the words and making them personal to your life and your journey.

This journal was created with you in mind. It is for the person who is seeking growth, development, and life improvement; the person who is ready and willing to take a personal inner journey. This journal is more than just specific affirmations. Rather, it was designed to facilitate your personalized experience by encouraging you to reflect and embark on an inner journey within yourself. As you work through this journal, you will be encouraged to explore your inner world, helping you to gain new insights and perspectives.

This is your personal journal, use it as a tool for self-discovery and paradigm-shifting as it pertains to soul healing, relationships, transformation, and success. There are 22 reflective affirmations per section. There is no order or timeframe to complete the journal. Work with what resonates with you through your life's journey.

"When we create peace and harmony and balance in our minds, we will find it in our lives."

- Louise Hay

Inner Reflections Affirmations Journey
Section One:
Affirmations for Soul Healing

I live my truths and stand on what I believe.

Write your personal truths and beliefs.

Ask yourself, do you live your personal truths? If not, why not?

Write out how you live your personal truths and stand for your beliefs.

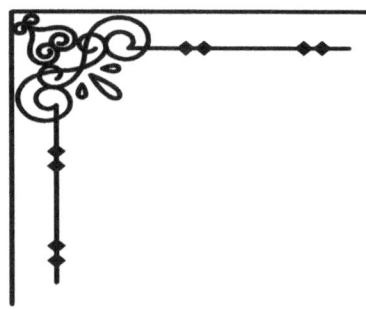

My soul is on a journey of greatness.

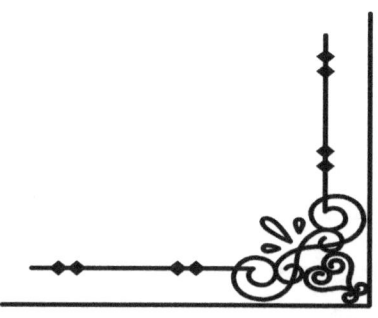

List ten ways in which you are great and boundless.

I am confidently walking on my soul's path.

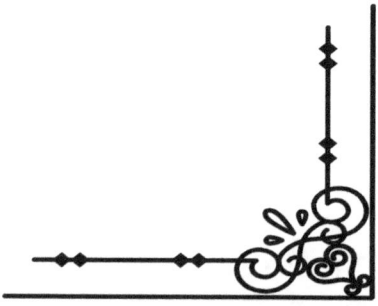

Reflect on life and congratulate yourself for honoring your soul's path.

Write out how you will continue to walk boldly and honor yourself.

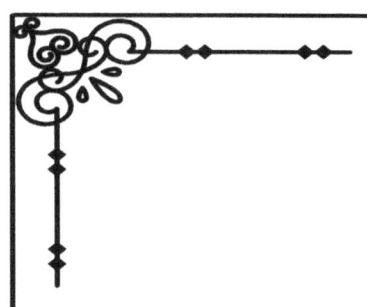

I am not my body.
My body is a vessel for my soul.

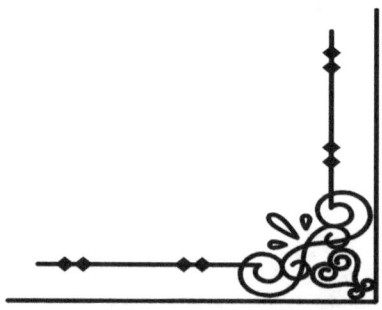

What does this affirmation mean to you?

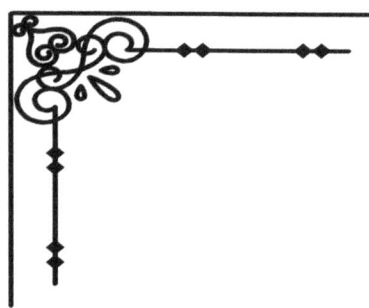

My relationship with myself is my most important relationship.

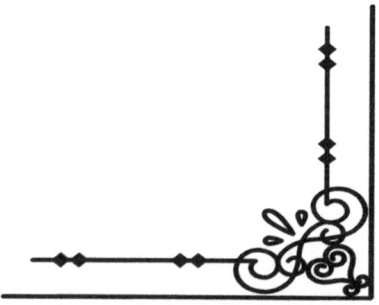

On a scale from 1 to 10, with 1 being the lowest (non-loving) and 10 being the highest (loving), how is your relationship with yourself?

How does the relationship you have with yourself compare to the relationships you have with others?

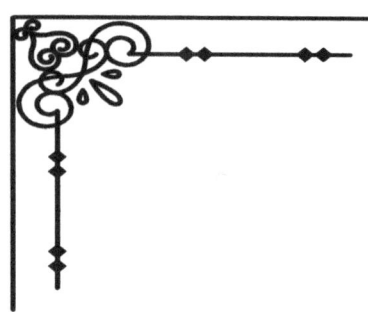

I unconditionally love and accept myself.

Write a list of at least ten things you love about yourself.

Write out five areas of your life that you should give more attention and love to.

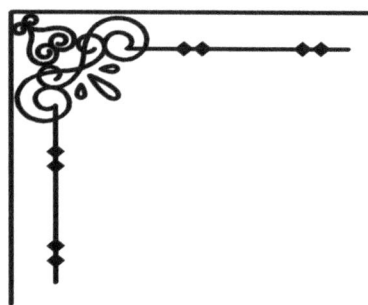

I am appreciated and loved.

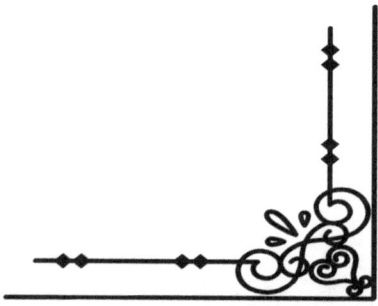

Reflect on, and write down, ten ways you express your love
and show your appreciation to yourself and to others.

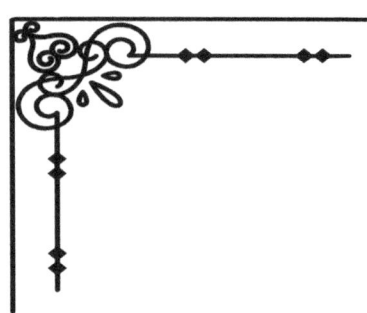

**I have unlimited potential.
I am a divine creator.**

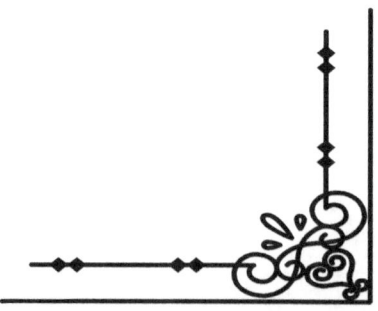

Envision what you desire to create, and write out
your vision with as much detail as possible.

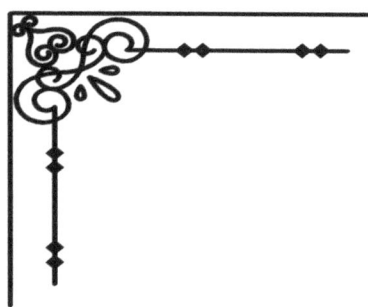

I can fully express myself and how I feel, even if it makes people feel uncomfortable.

Write out all the ways you express yourself.

(Writing, singing, dancing, talking, drawing, etc.).

Do you suppress or deny yourself from expressing yourself or your feelings?
If so, why and how can you start expressing yourself more?

_____
_____
_____
_____
_____
_____
_____
_____
_____
_____
_____
_____
_____

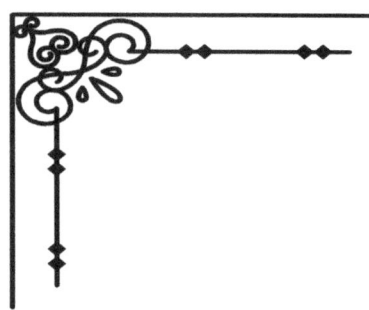

I am ready to heal my mind, body, and soul. My emotional health is as important as my physical health.

Reflect on your emotional health and write down five ways you can improve your emotional wellness.

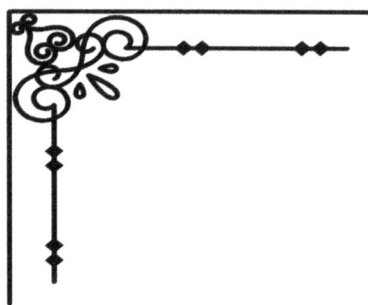

Healing is a process!

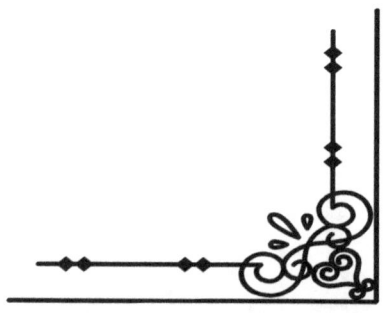

Write the top three areas of your life that you are ready to heal.

What actions or steps will you take today to start your healing process?

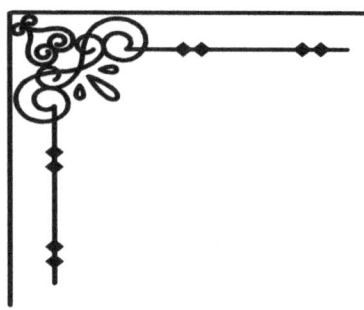

**I can fulfill my emotional needs;
I am the source of my happiness.**

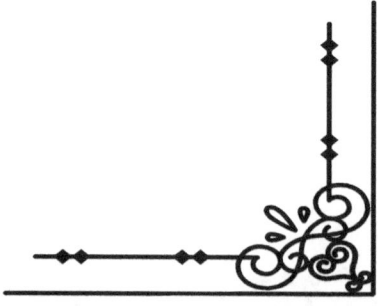

Our emotional needs stem from our childhoods.
What are your top three emotional needs?
How can you meet those needs?

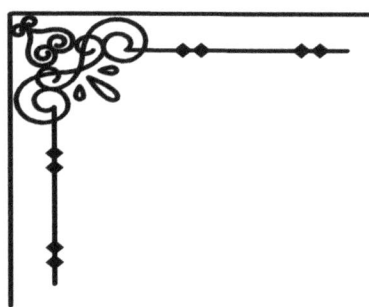

**I choose to heal from
my emotional wounds.**

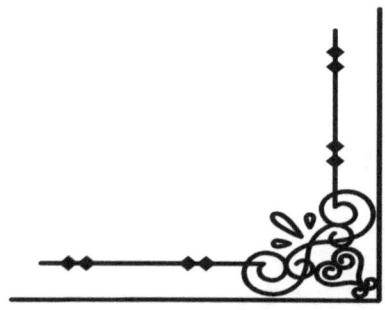

Emotional wounds are just as painful as physical wounds, perhaps even more so. What emotional wounds do you need to heal?

How will you feel once your wounds are healed?

_____
_____
_____
_____
_____
_____
_____
_____
_____
_____
_____
_____
_____
_____
_____

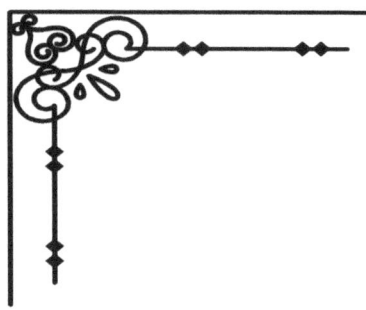

My feelings are valid; I accept my feelings as messages to myself to pay attention to what is occurring within myself and my environment.

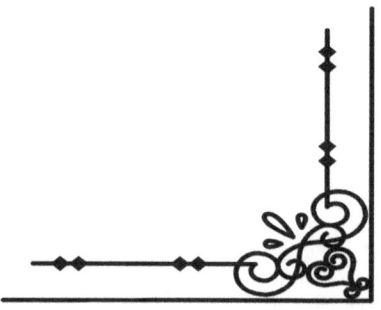

Our feelings are like signposts; they are our guiding system.
Are your aware of your feelings and what they are attempting to communicate to you?

What are your most common feelings? Are they positive, negative, or neutral?

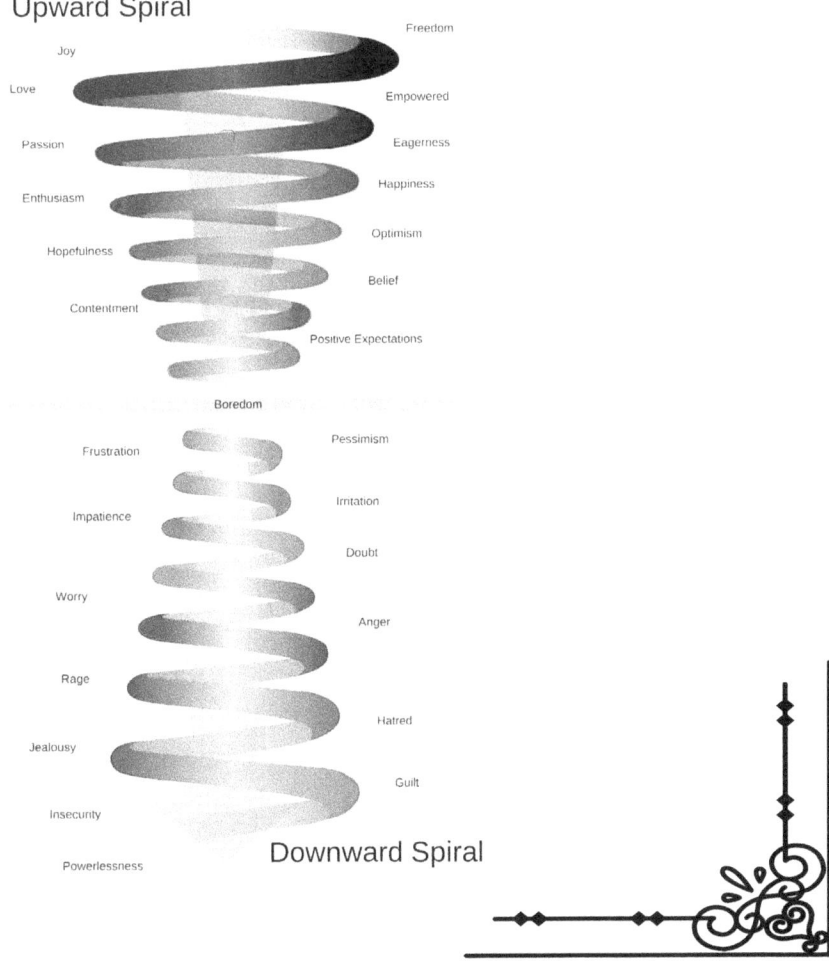

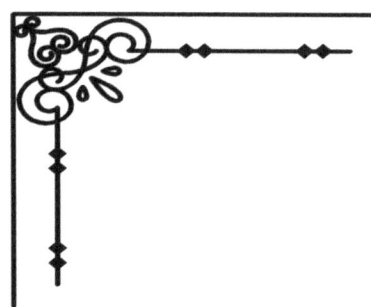

I am free to release any repressed negative emotions.

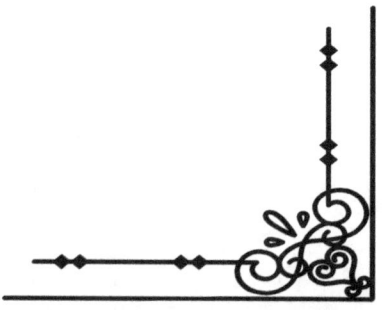

Reflect on the causes of any unpleasant emotions you commonly experience.

What is the source of these unpleasant emotions?

How can do start today to begin releasing unwanted emotions?

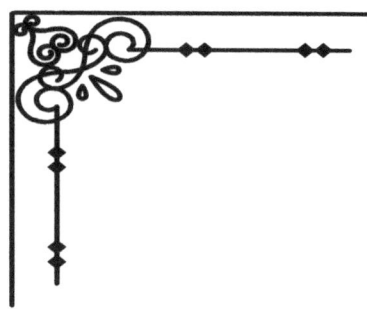

I have the right to protect my personal boundaries.

Reflect on your physical and emotional boundaries.

How do you protect and maintain your boundaries?

If your boundaries need strengthening, list out how you can develop healthy personal boundaries.

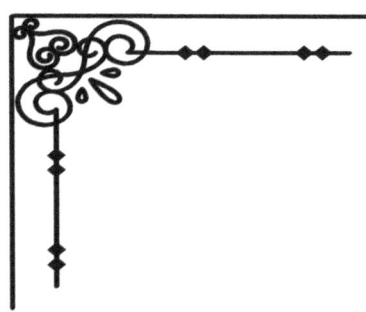

I have the right to say "NO" to what I do not want!

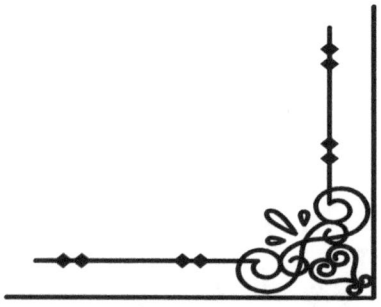

Why do you say "yes" when you really want to say "no"?

How does saying "no" make you feel?

Start today, by saying "no" to what you do not want.

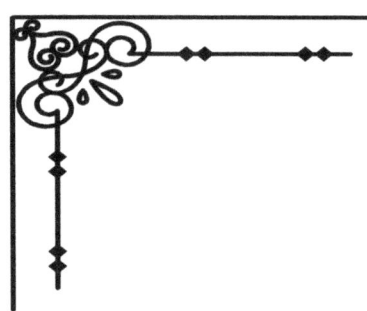

I have the right to say "yes" to what I do want!

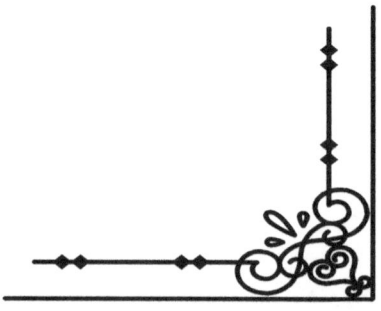

Why do you say "no" when you really want to say "yes"?

How does saying "yes" make you feel?

Start today, saying "yes" to what you really want.

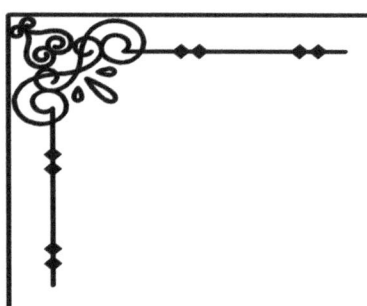

I forgive those who have caused me harm.

To forgive is to release past hurt and pain anchored to someone else.
To forgive is to give yourself permission to live again.

Write a list of all the people you need to forgive,
and begin to forgive them, one by one.

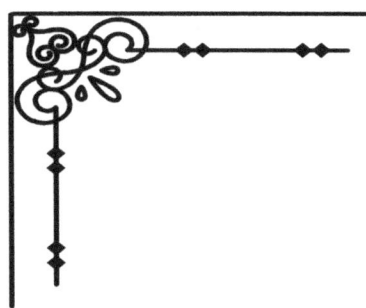

I forgive myself.

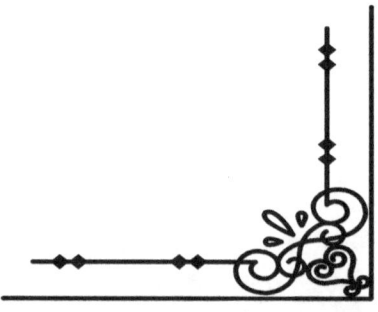

Reflect over your life. Are you punishing yourself?
Do you need to forgive yourself?

Write out what you need to forgive yourself for.
I forgive myself for…

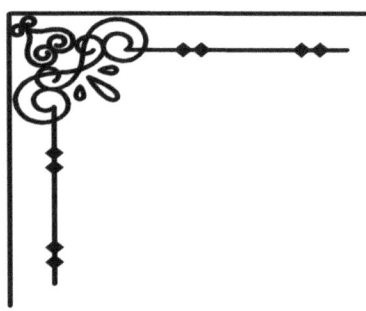

I deserve to experience the best life has to offer.

What is it that you would like to experience, and you know you deserve?

Are you holding yourself back? If so, why and how can you change your experiences?

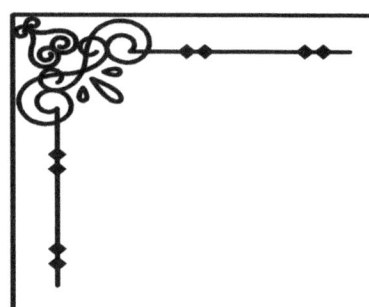

I am entitled to be happy and enjoy my life.

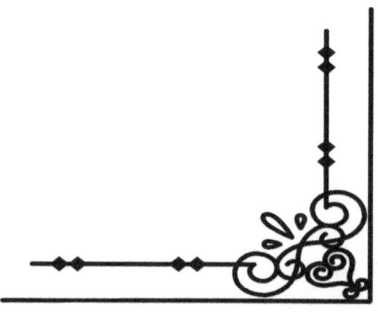

What brings you the most enjoyment and happiness in your life?

Is there anything additional you can do to increase joy in your life?

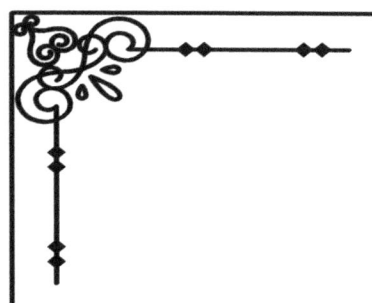

Additional Insights

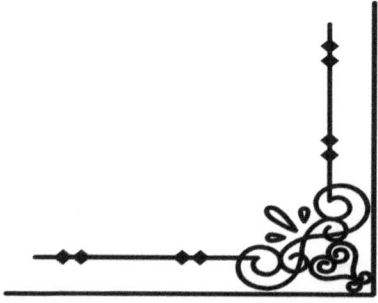

Personal relationships are the fertile soil from which all advancement, all success, all achievement in real life grows.

- Ben Stein

Inner Reflections Affirmations Journey
Section Two:

Affirmations for Relationships

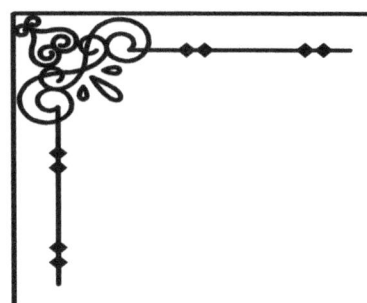

I am an expression of love.

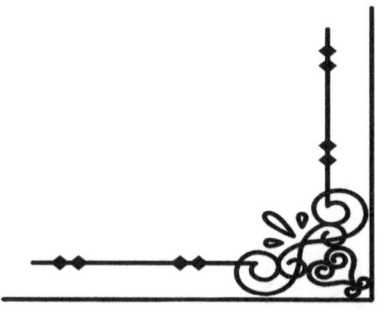

Love is expressed through the heart.

Do you express your love from your mind or your heart?

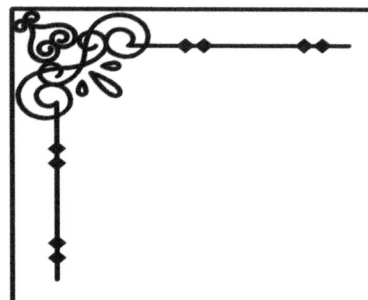

I am open to receiving love and affection.

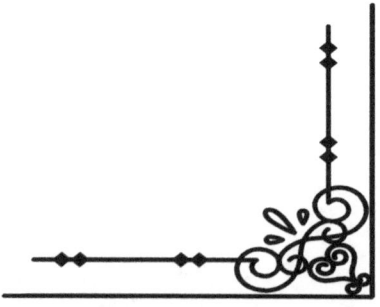

Is there anything blocking you from accepting love and affection from others? If so, what is it?

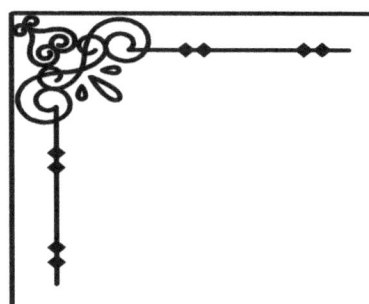

I am committed to nurturing and enhancing my relationship.

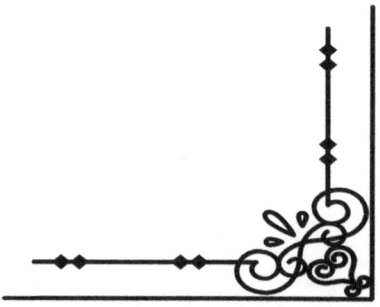

Relationships grow when they're nurtured.

What are five ways you can nurture and enhance your relationship?

I present my best self in my relationship.

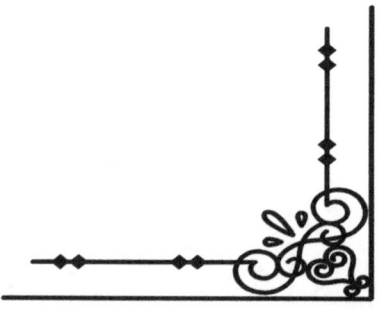

Have you become too comfortable in your relationship?
Have you stopped doing the little things that initially fueled the relationship?
Your relationship deserves the best "You" you can give.

Write out your thoughts about your relationship and how you can present your best self in the relationship.

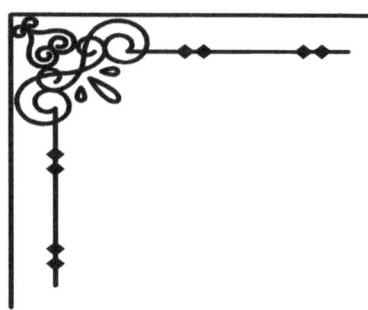

I love being intimate with my significant other and expressing myself through affection.

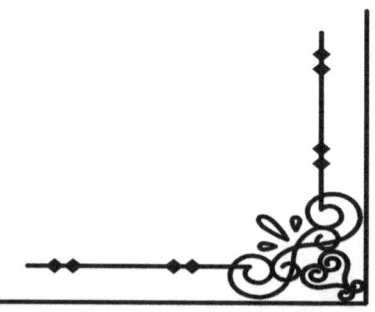

Affection is one way of showing that you care and that the love is still brewing.

What are five ways you are affectionate with your partner?

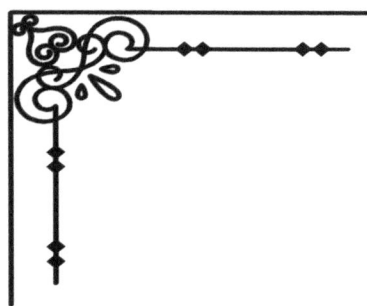

I enjoy being intimate.

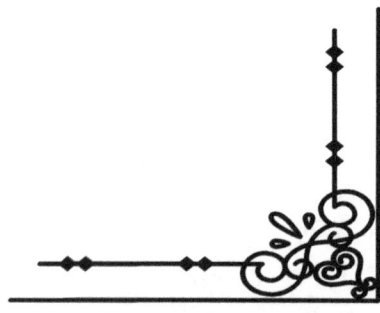

Intimacy is more than physical contact; it entails spiritual, mental, and emotional connections.

How intimate are you with your significant other on a scale from 1 to 10? In what ways can you deepen the intimacy within your relationship?

___

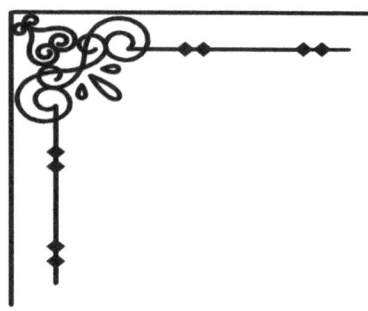

I am emotionally mature and communicate my needs and wants directly to my significant other.

What are the three most important needs and wants you desire from your significant other?

Are you willing to communicate these needs and wants?

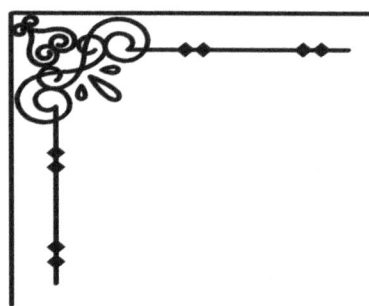

I am supportive and understanding of my partner's needs.

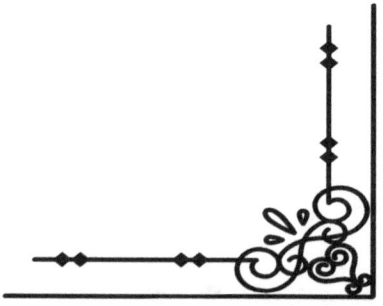

Take a moment to reflect on how you support your partner and their needs within the relationship.

Are any changes needed? If so, what needs to change?

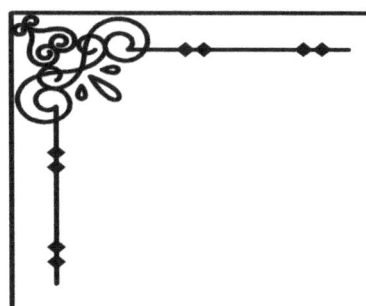

I am spiritually connected to my love and, together, we create the life we desire to live.

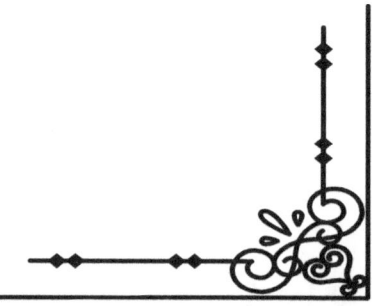

In detail, write out your vision of the future you desire to experience with your love.

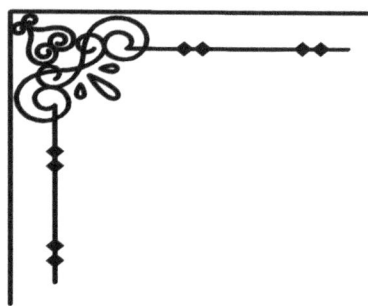

My relationship helps me to become consciously aware of myself.

Your relationship is a mirror of yourself, your subconscious being.

What is your relationship reflecting to you, about you?

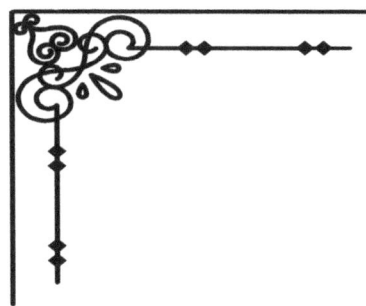

My relationship is constantly evolving. I am aware relationships expand and grow with active participation.

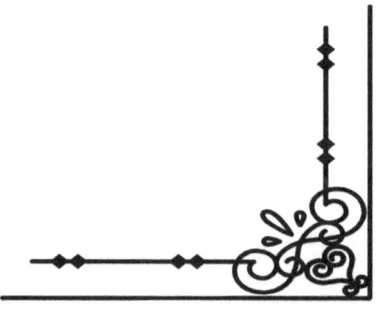

Choose to actively participate in your relationship with compassion and love.

In what areas can your relationship grow?

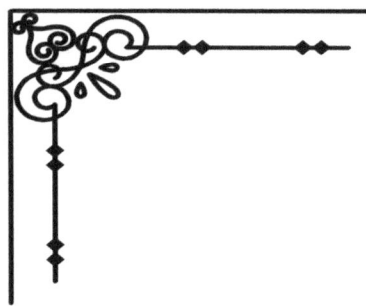

I will continue to find ways to maintain romance in my relationship.

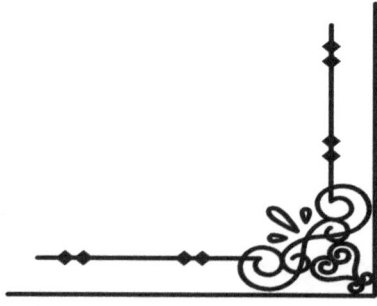

How do you define romance?

Write out a list of new things you are willing to do to enhance and maintain romance in your relationship.

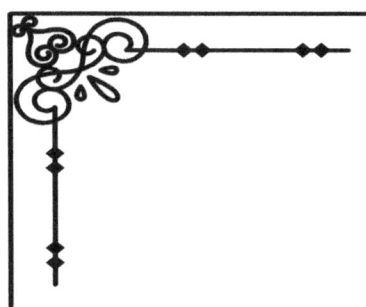

I am responsible for communicating my needs to my partner.

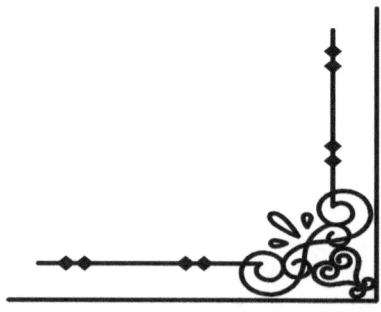

Is there anything that you need to communicate to your partner, but have not? If so, what is blocking the communication flow?

What are three things you need to communicate to your partner now?

___
___
___
___
___
___
___
___
___
___
___
___
___
___
___

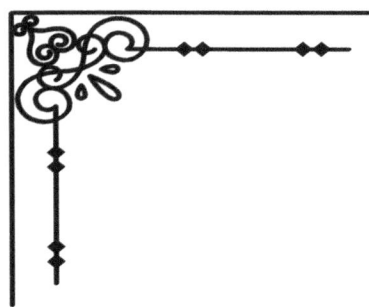

I am gaining a greater understanding of myself and my partner.

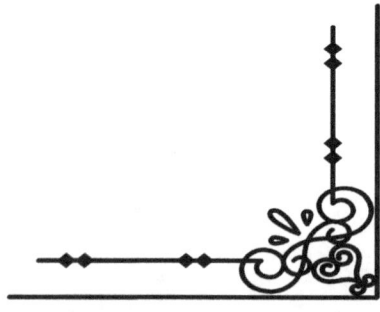

Individually, we are constantly evolving and so are our relationships. How do you think you and your partner have evolved during your relationship?

What are the three most significant things you have learned about yourself and your partner during your relationship?

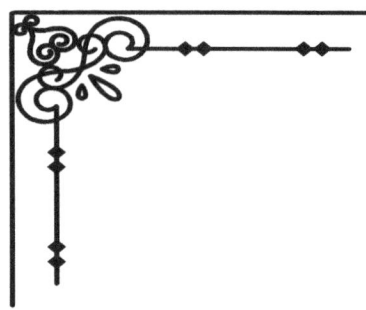

I accept my significant other's past, and I accept them as they are today.

We all have a past, and no one can change their past.
Love your partner as they are now.

What do you need to accept about your past, or about yourself?
What do you need to accept about your partner?

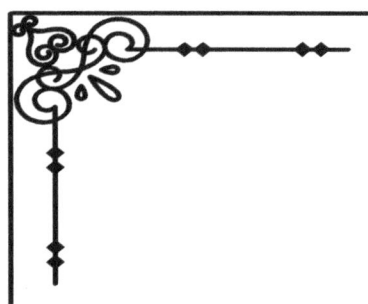

I am thoughtful and considerate of my partner's needs.

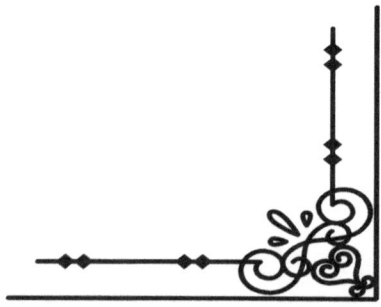

How do you express appreciation for your partner?

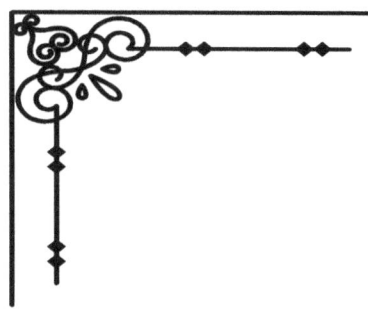

I am patient.

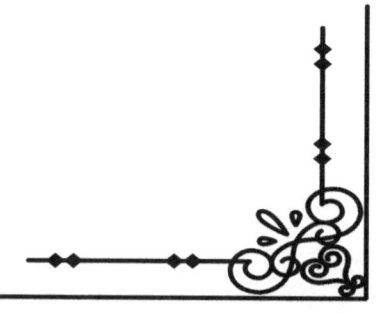

Write the five areas where you can develop more patience
with yourself and within your relationship.

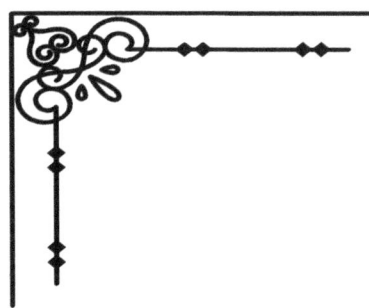

I am developing an unbreakable bond with my partner.

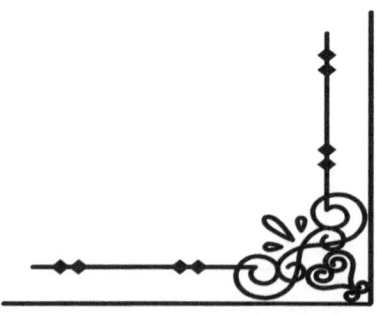

The connection and bond you have with your partner should be unmatched.

Reflect on the connection and bond you have with your partner.

In what ways can you make the bond stronger?

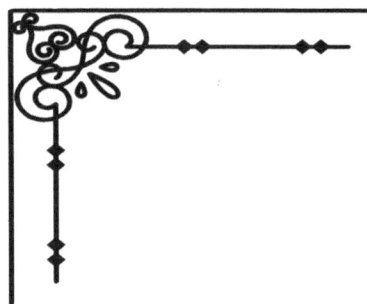

I am deserving of a loving relationship.

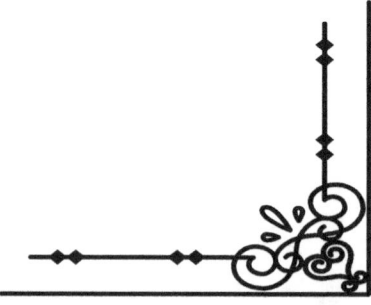

If you are experiencing a less-than-loving relationship, ask yourself why. Do you believe you deserve a loving relationship?

Write down ten reasons you deserve to be in a loving relationship.

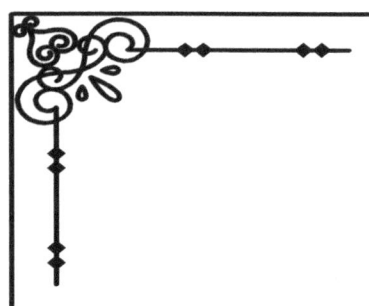

I am striving for a balanced and well-nurtured relationship.

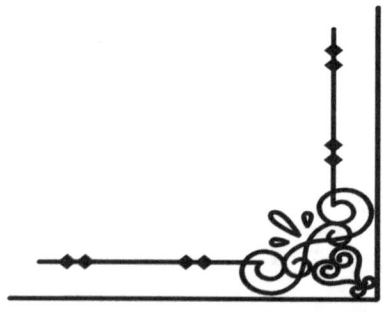

In what ways do you, or can you, contribute to your relationship to maintain harmony?

**I am responsible for creating
the relationship I wish to experience.**

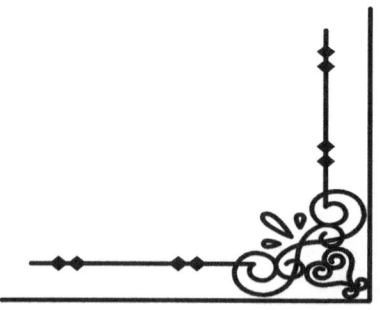

Write out how you are taking responsibility for creating the relationship you desire.

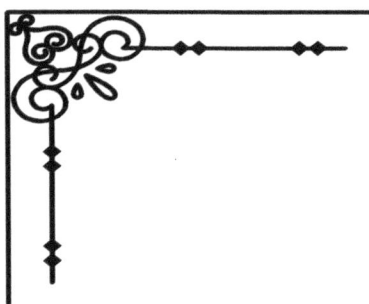

I am growing in my relationship.

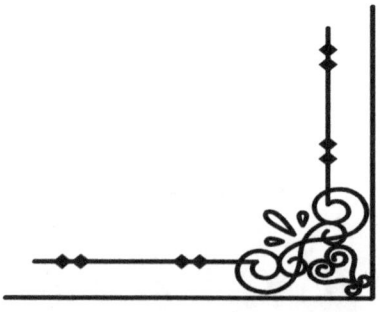

Relationships help you to grow and develop as a person. Do not be afraid to expand within your relationship.

Do you feel that you are expanding as a person?

Does your relationship promote self-development and improvement?

Reflect on your relationship, does it create space for personal growth?

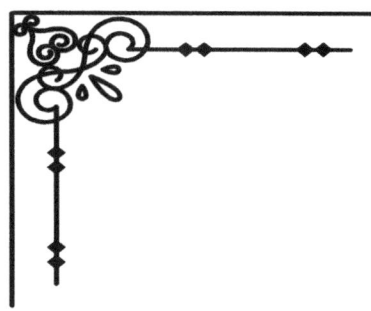

Additional Insights

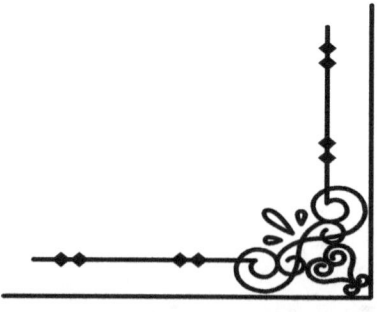

"Nothing happens until the pain of remaining the same outweighs the pain of change."

~Arthur Burt

Inner Reflections Affirmations Journey
Section Three:

Affirmations for Transformation

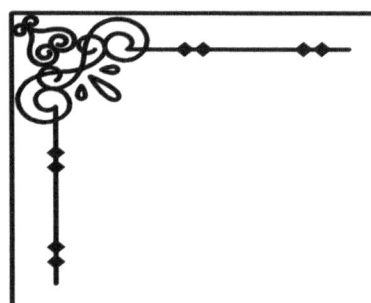

I am powerful! This situation is unfamiliar to me, but I will overcome any challenges that I face head-on!

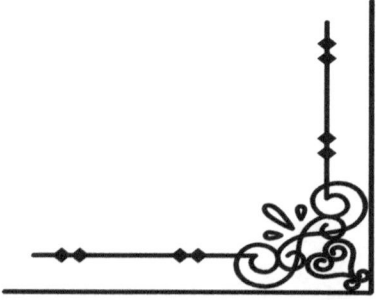

Write out how you have dealt with challenges in the past and how you plan to boldly face any new challenges you encounter.

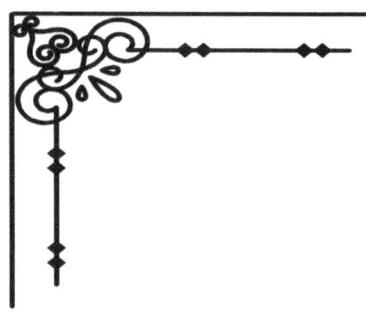

I am moving forward; my past is behind me now. I am entering into a new and exciting life experience.

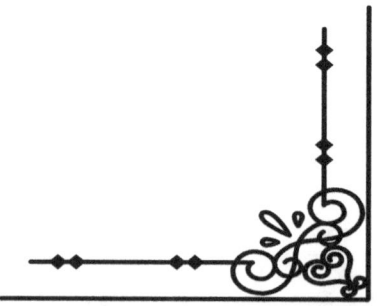

Are you ready for a new experience?

As of this moment, what are you ready to create and experience in your life?

_____
_____
_____
_____
_____
_____
_____
_____
_____
_____
_____
_____
_____
_____
_____
_____

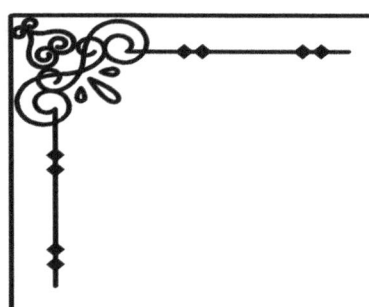

This is the beginning of something new in my life, and I'm excited about what is in store.

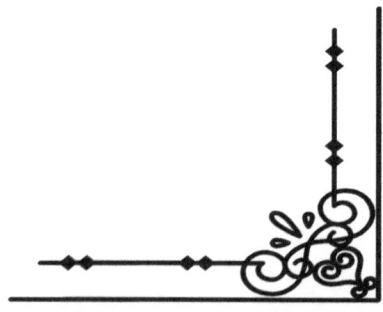

As one chapter ends, another begins.

If you were to create the "perfect" life for yourself, what would it entail?
Write the details out as if you were writing a story.

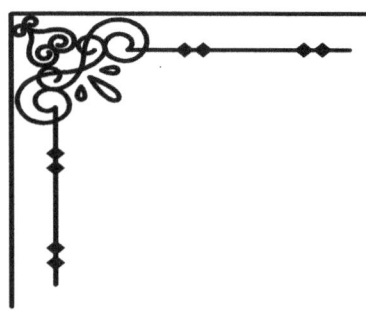

I welcome this new phase of my life with open arms.

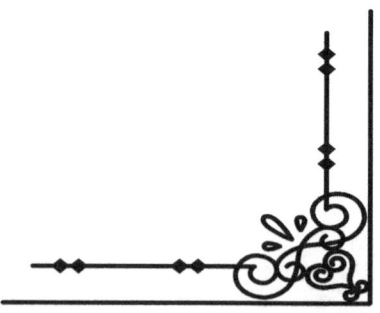

It is hard to receive with closed arms.

How are you positioning yourself to receive and enter into the next phase of your life?

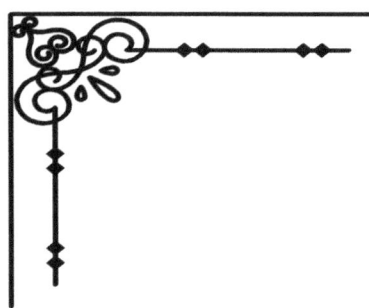

**I am stronger today than
I was yesterday.**

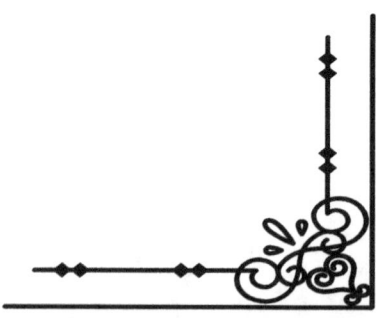

Reflect on yesterday and write how you are stronger and greater today.

How will you be even stronger and greater tomorrow?

My yesterday will not be my tomorrow.

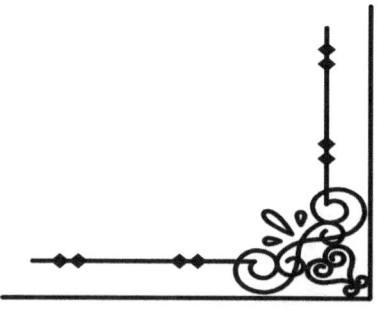

You have the ability to change what you do not want in your life.

What do you need to change now, so that you do not repeat your unwanted past?

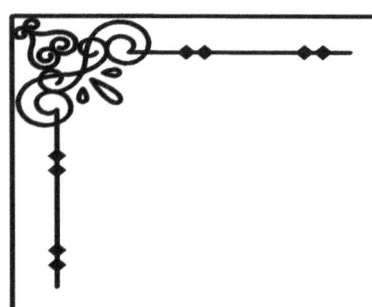

Every day, I am making my life better and better.

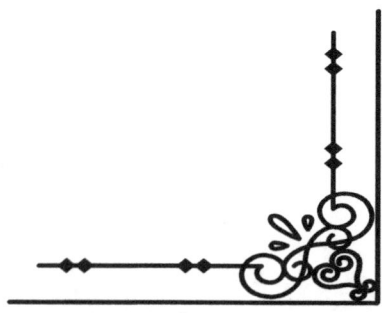

Write out five ways you are making your life better, now and for the future.

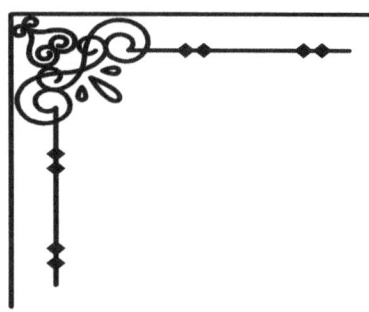

I will remain calm during this time of uncertainty, and I will focus on what I can control.

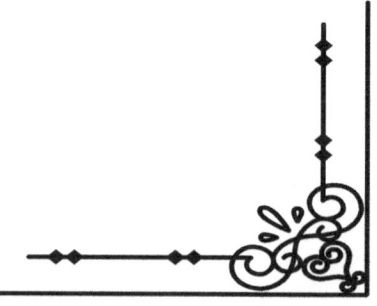

Focus on what you can control.

Reflect over your life; identify and write down what you can and what you cannot control within your life or your current circumstance.

_____
_____
_____
_____
_____
_____
_____
_____
_____
_____
_____
_____
_____
_____
_____

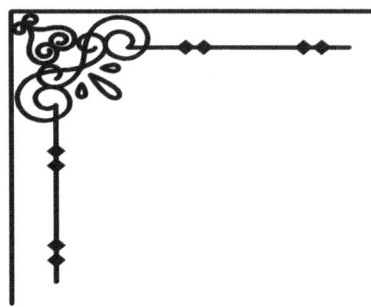

Today I will take it one hour at a time.
I will focus on staying in the
present moment.

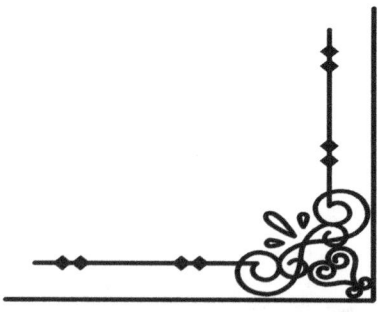

Take three deep breaths and notice your environment.

In this present moment, what are you experiencing?

**Tomorrow is not promised, so today,
I will live my best life.**

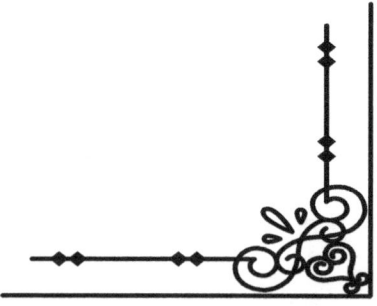

If today was your last opportunity to achieve or experience something, what would you do?

Why have you not done it yet?

Write out a plan to achieve this goal or to have this experience.

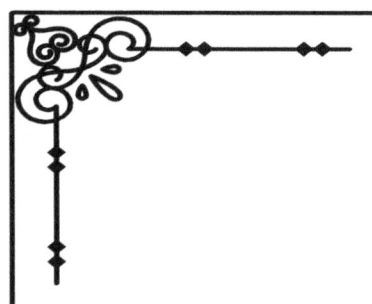

I have learned and grown from my past mistakes. I am not my mistakes.

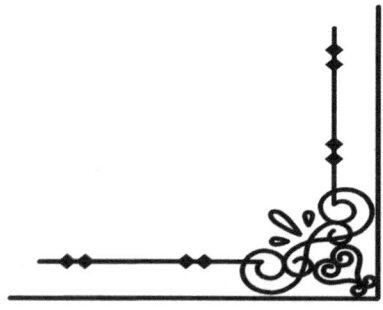

Mistakes simply mean you have misstepped.

Now, you have learned what not to do. You are not your mistakes because you are still in the process of learning and growing.

Write three "mistakes" that helped you grow into the person you are now.

_____
_____
_____
_____
_____
_____
_____
_____
_____
_____
_____
_____
_____

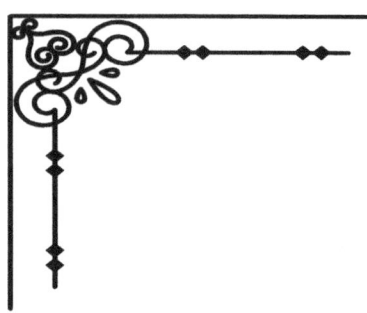

**I am totally responsible for how I respond to life.
I am responsible for my life.**

You have total control over yourself and what you create.

As a person of power, you take responsibility for what you do and say and for what you do not do or say.

How do you take full responsibility for your life?

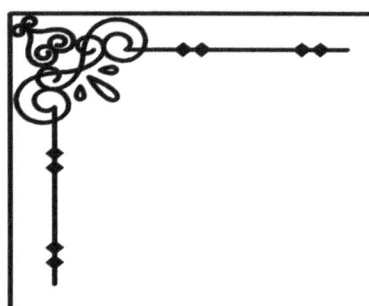

I choose to remove myself from situations that no longer serve me.

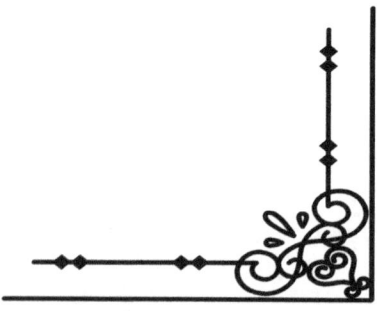

Identify situation(s) in your life that no longer serve you.

List the situation(s) and state why it is no longer fitting for your life.

I will release people from my life who are no longer in alignment with me.

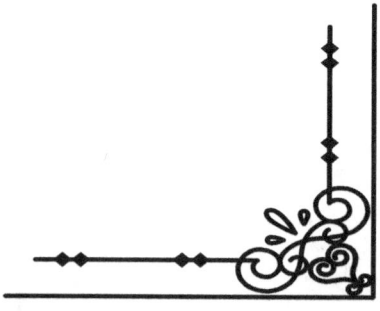

Not everyone can go where you are heading.

Make a list of people you feel are no longer in alignment with you and your vision and release them with love.

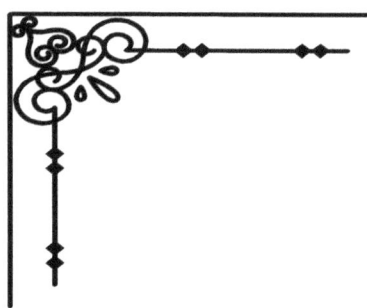

This situation is temporary; it is allowing me to gain a greater understanding of myself and my life.

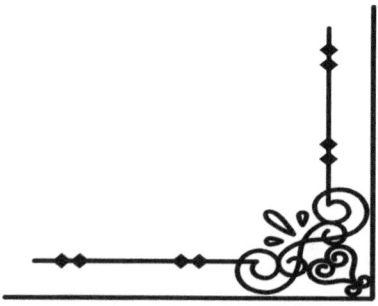

Write down what your current situation is teaching you about yourself, your life, and your desires.

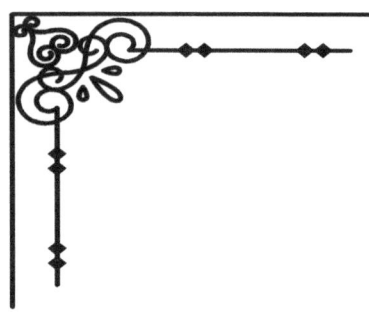

I have gained valuable lessons from my past that I will use to create a successful future.

What are the two most valuable lessons that you have learned from your past?

How will you implement what you've learned from those experiences to create success in the future?

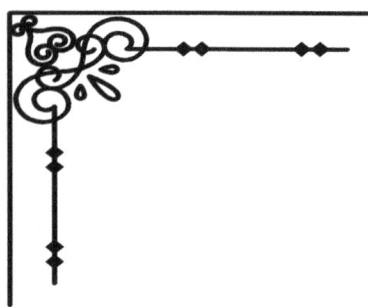

I am learning and growing through this transition.

What has your most recent transition taught you about yourself,
your life, and how you view life?

I am ready to learn more about myself, to connect more with myself, and to expand myself during this experience.

How will your recent life experience enhance your life overall?

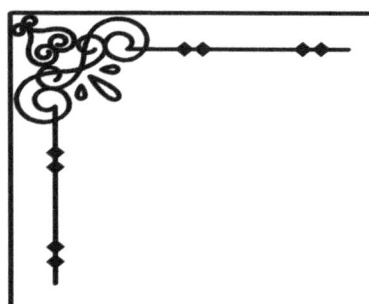

I am undergoing a transformation, and I understand that it is a process.

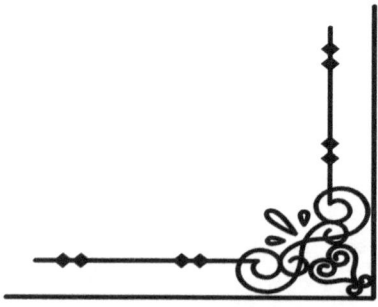

Transformation equals change.

How can you navigate through this change and embrace the transformation in a way that will be the most beneficial to you?

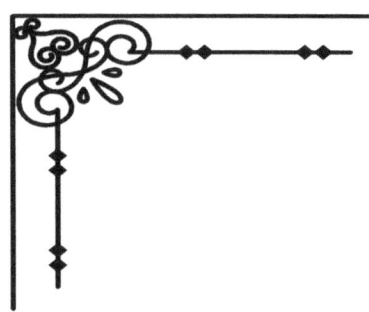

I am expanding and evolving my mind; I am changing for the better.

Are your thoughts positive and uplifting?

Take some time to reflect on your thoughts.

Write seven positive things about yourself, your life, and your current situation.

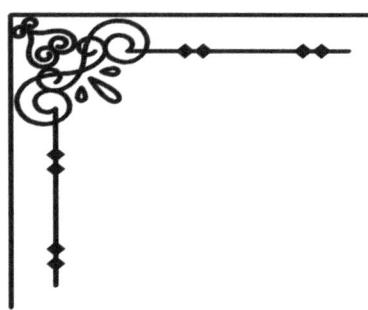

I am developing mental, emotional, and spiritual strength as I undergo this life change.

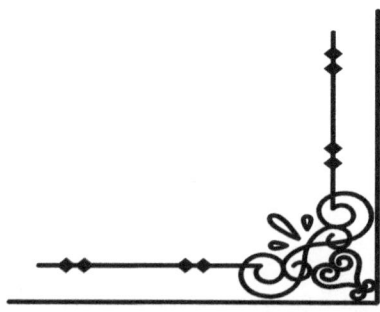

Write out how you have gained mental, emotional,
and spiritual strength as you have undergone life changes.

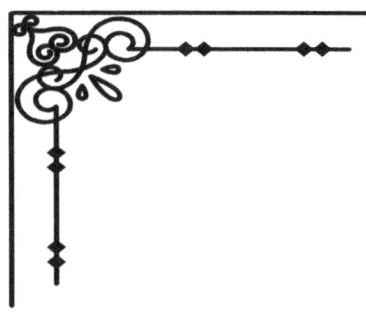

I know that change is uncomfortable; however, this change is for the betterment of my life.

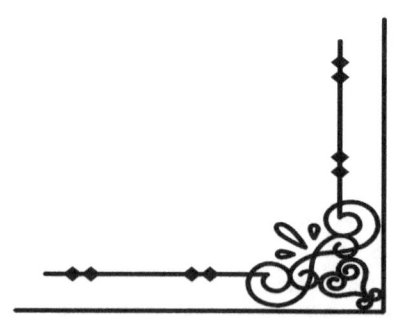

Embrace this change.

What is the most uncomfortable part of this change?

How can this change improve your life?

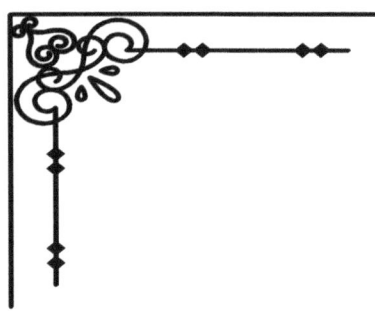

Additional Insights

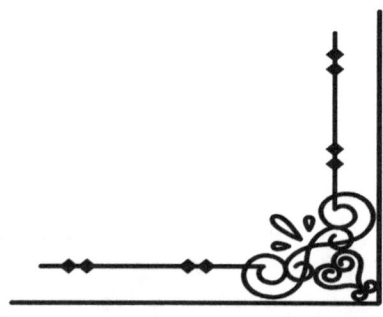

Every adversity, every failure, every heartache carries with it the seed of an equal or greater benefit.

- Napoleon Hill

Inner Reflections Affirmations Journey Section Four:

Affirmations for Success

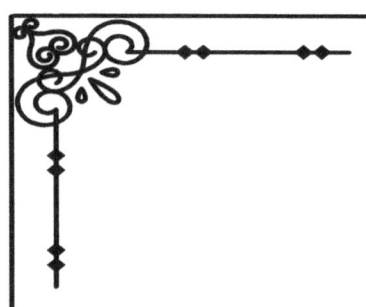

I am victorious! I have the mental, emotional, and physical strength to win this battle.

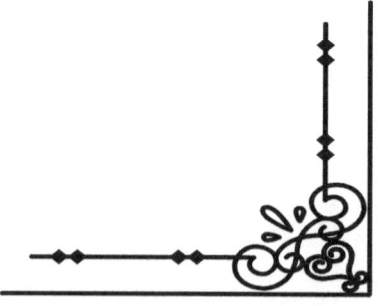

List the strengths that enable you to be victorious.

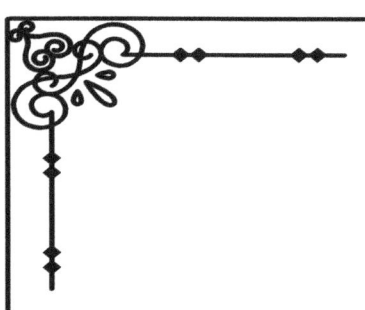

**I am excited! I am enthusiastic!
I am passionate!**

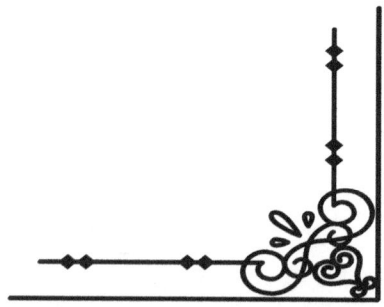

Always remember your "why" and why you started.

Write out your passions and how you are pursuing them.

If you are not pursuing your passions, what do you need to do to start?

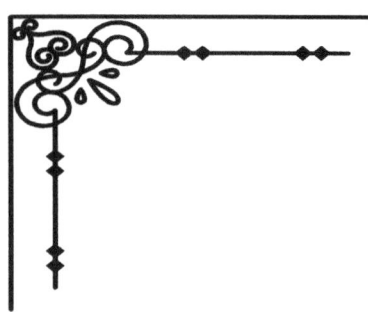

I am worthy of love, respect, and happiness.

How does knowing you are worthy of love, respect,
and happiness contribute to your success?

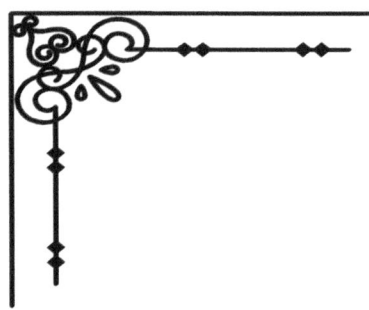

I know my purpose, and I am alive to fulfill that purpose.

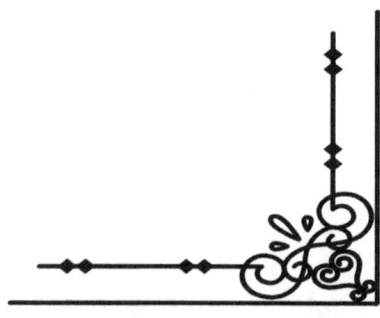

What is your purpose, both personally and professionally?

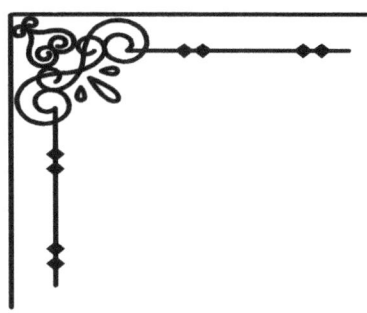

I am willing to move out of my comfort zone and expand my life's experiences and perspectives.

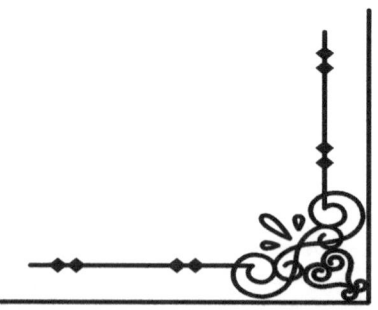

What is preventing you from getting out of your comfort zone?

If you are out of your comfort zone, what is the next major goal or event that will stretch you beyond your "new" comfort zone?

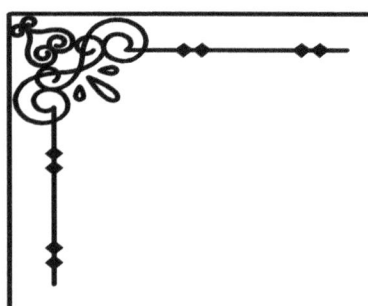

I have a clear vision, and I will see my vision manifest.

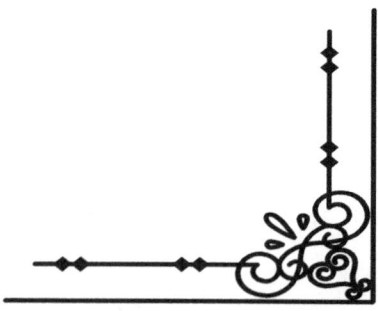

Document your life vision and view it often.

Set an impression in your mind, on both the conscious and subconscious levels.

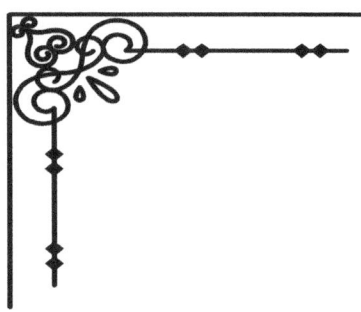

I am ready and available for any opportunity that presents itself in pursuit of achieving my goals.

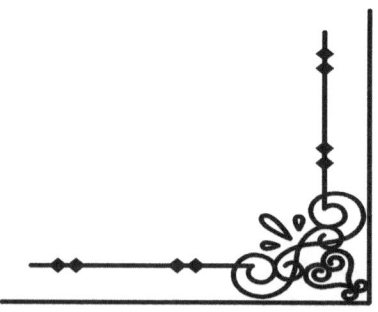

What opportunities are you prepared to explore now, to achieve your goals?

If you are not ready, what do you need to do to get focused and ready for the next opportunity that is presented to you?

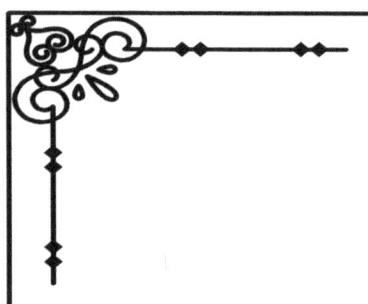

I will continue to work towards my goals and will achieve them all.

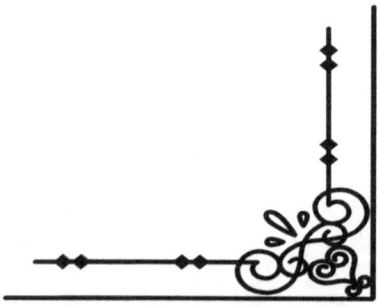

When you are faced with challenges and obstacles on the way to achieving your goals, what skills will you use to continue pushing forward?

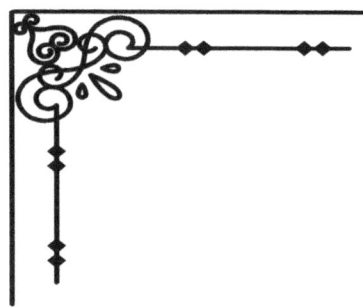

I am passionate about my goals, and I will achieve each one with ease.

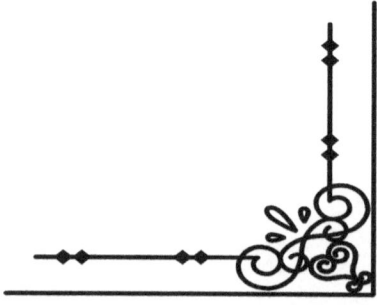

What are your goals? Write your goals out ten times below.

Repetition makes an imprint upon your subconscious mind.

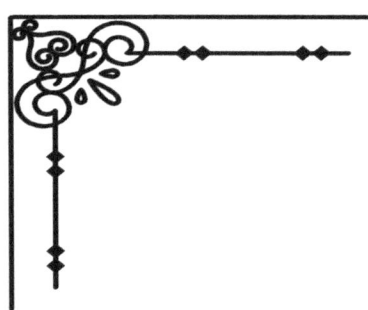

I will focus my attention on efforts that will move me closer to achieving my goals.

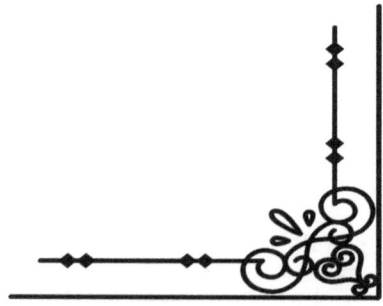

What is currently distracting you from focusing on achieving your goals?

What are you doing to minimize, or remove the identified distractions?

I accept failure as a temporary setback. Ultimately, it will add to my success.

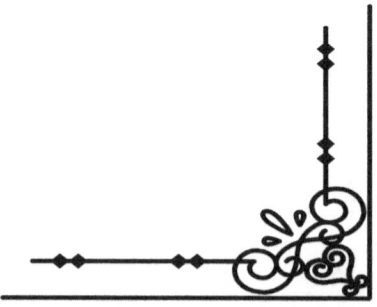

Failures are opportunities to learn what does not work.

Failures are stepping stones to your success.

Are you afraid to fail? If so, why?

Write out your thoughts and feelings surrounding failure and how to use your past failures as lessons for the future.

_____
_____
_____
_____
_____
_____
_____
_____
_____
_____
_____
_____
_____

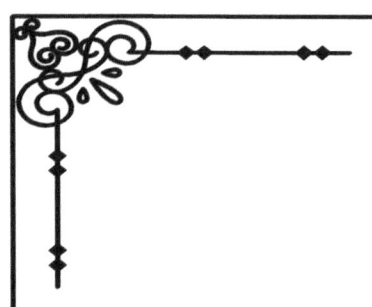

I am efficient and produce above-average results.

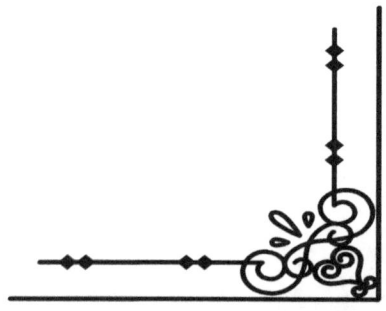

What above average results are you producing?

How are you operating with excellence?

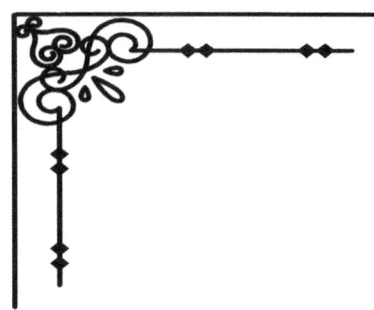

I am talented.

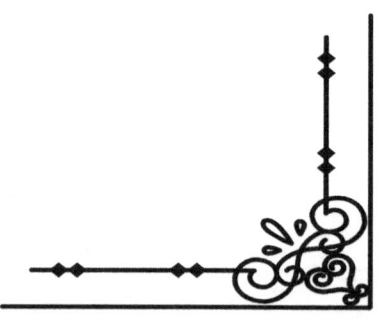

What are three talents that separate you from others?

How are you using these talents within your life?

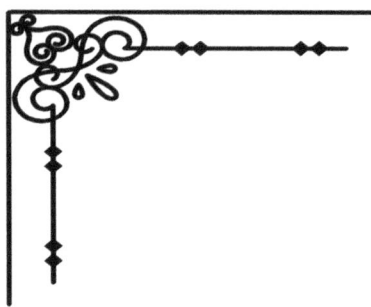

I am successful.

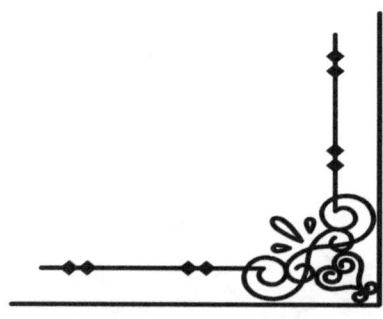

Write down all the areas of your life in which you are successful.

Which areas need more attention?

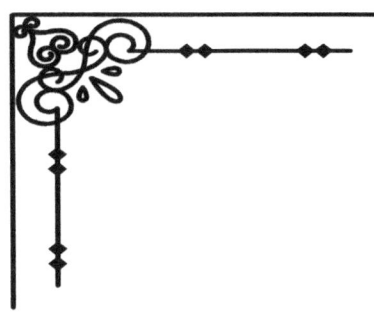

I define my success.

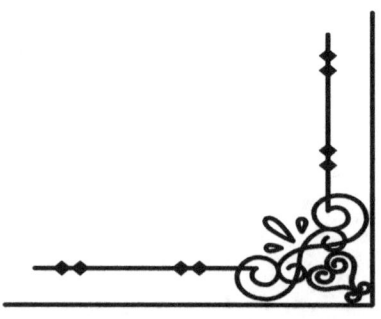

What is your definition of success?

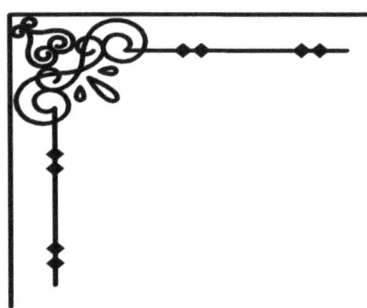

I will achieve my goals, step by step.

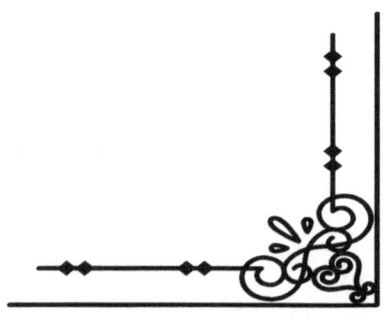

There are no shortcuts to success.

Are you willing and ready to take the road to success?

What are the known steps you must take to achieve the success you desire?

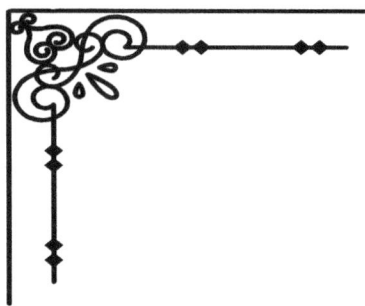

I am so thankful for my success.

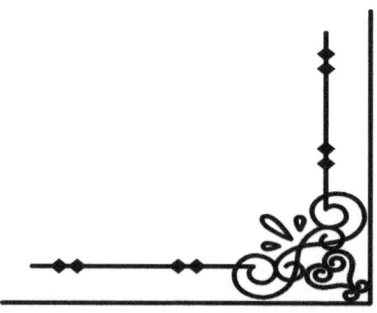

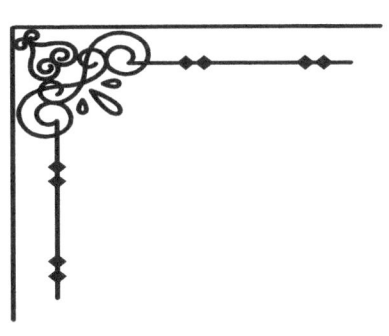

Make a gratitude list for your success:

I am so thankful for….

I am so grateful that…

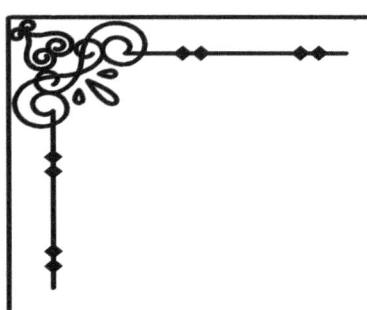

I evoke feelings of success;
I am wise, mentally resilient,
and fully capable of winning.

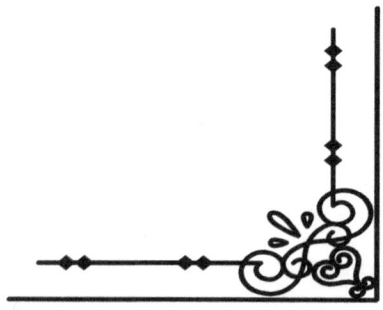

Write out ten ways you are resilient and maintain your mental agility.

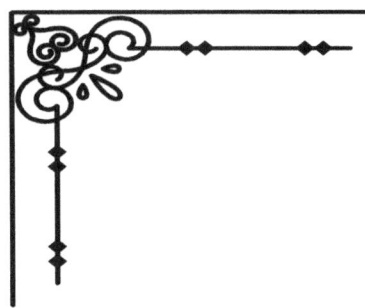

I give myself permission to excel.

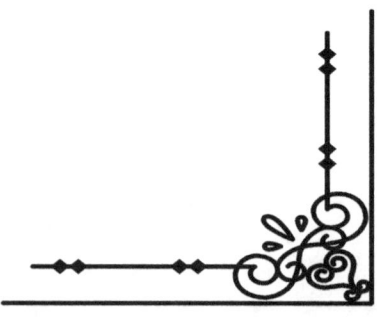

Envision yourself at the summit, the peak of success, and write out the experience in detail.

What does it feel like to excel, to be at the top?

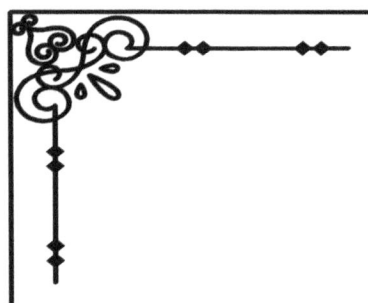

I am disciplined; I have determination.

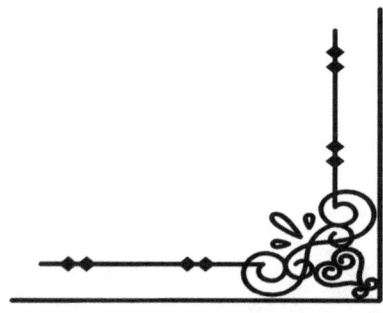

How do you use your mindset to accomplish your goals?

Describe your discipline and determination.

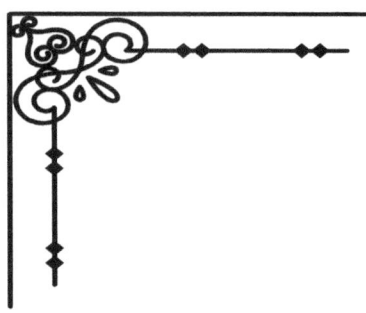

I am open to continuous growth and personal development on the road to my success.

Learning is a lifelong process, and self-development is a continuous process.

What are you currently doing, or what can you do, to enhance your life and further develop yourself?

_____
_____
_____
_____
_____
_____
_____
_____
_____
_____
_____
_____
_____
_____
_____

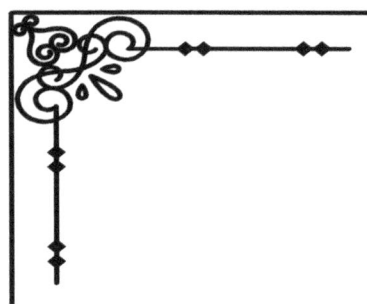

I am proud of myself and all that I have achieved thus far in my life.

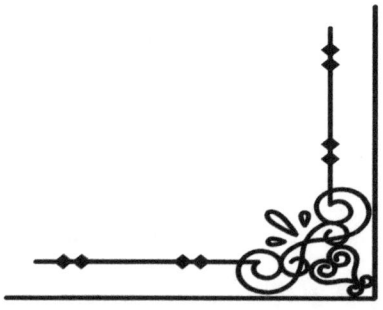

Reflect on your achievements.

List your top three and describe how you felt at the time.

Are you ready to achieve more? Are you ready to achieve something greater?

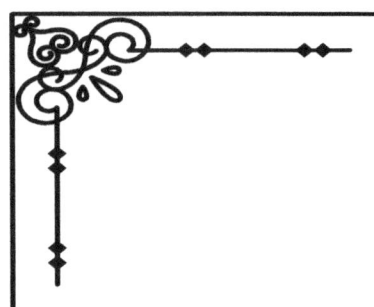

Additional Insights

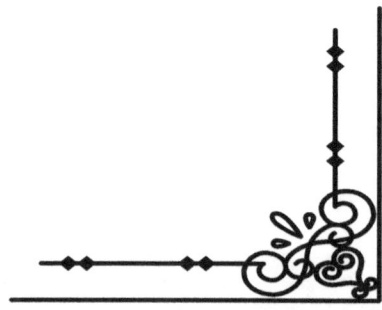

SAY IT, BELIEVE IT, BE IT

www.ingramcontent.com/pod-product-compliance
Lightning Source LLC
Chambersburg PA
CBHW081108080526
44587CB00021B/3504